BEI GRIN MACHT SICH IHR WISSEN BEZAHLT

- Wir veröffentlichen Ihre Hausarbeit, Bachelor- und Masterarbeit

- Ihr eigenes eBook und Buch - weltweit in allen wichtigen Shops

- Verdienen Sie an jedem Verkauf

Jetzt bei www.GRIN.com hochladen und kostenlos publizieren

Bibliografische Information der Deutschen Nationalbibliothek:

Die Deutsche Bibliothek verzeichnet diese Publikation in der Deutschen Nationalbibliografie; detaillierte bibliografische Daten sind im Internet über http://dnb.d-nb.de/ abrufbar.

Dieses Werk sowie alle darin enthaltenen einzelnen Beiträge und Abbildungen sind urheberrechtlich geschützt. Jede Verwertung, die nicht ausdrücklich vom Urheberrechtsschutz zugelassen ist, bedarf der vorherigen Zustimmung des Verlages. Das gilt insbesondere für Vervielfältigungen, Bearbeitungen, Übersetzungen, Mikroverfilmungen, Auswertungen durch Datenbanken und für die Einspeicherung und Verarbeitung in elektronische Systeme. Alle Rechte, auch die des auszugsweisen Nachdrucks, der fotomechanischen Wiedergabe (einschließlich Mikrokopie) sowie der Auswertung durch Datenbanken oder ähnliche Einrichtungen, vorbehalten.

Impressum:

Copyright © 2017 GRIN Verlag
Druck und Bindung: Books on Demand GmbH, Norderstedt Germany
ISBN: 9783668718531

Dieses Buch bei GRIN:

https://www.grin.com/document/427495

Anonym

Fragen stellen und beantworten. Ein Interview mit einem Sportstar (Englisch 6. Klasse Gymnasium)

GRIN Verlag

GRIN - Your knowledge has value

Der GRIN Verlag publiziert seit 1998 wissenschaftliche Arbeiten von Studenten, Hochschullehrern und anderen Akademikern als eBook und gedrucktes Buch. Die Verlagswebsite www.grin.com ist die ideale Plattform zur Veröffentlichung von Hausarbeiten, Abschlussarbeiten, wissenschaftlichen Aufsätzen, Dissertationen und Fachbüchern.

Besuchen Sie uns im Internet:

http://www.grin.com/

http://www.facebook.com/grincom

http://www.twitter.com/grin_com

Kurzentwurf für den X. Unterrichtsbesuch im Fach Englisch

Datum:
Zeit:
Lerngruppe: 6
Raum:
Fachlehrerin:

Unterrichtlicher Zusammenhang

Thema der Unterrichtseinheit:	Unit 4: Sport is good for you!
Thema der vorausgegangenen Stunde:	Present Perfect – Have you ever…?
Thema der heutigen Stunde:	Fragen stellen und beantworten – An interview
Thema der nachfolgenden Stunde:	Present Perfect

Ziele der Stunde

Zentrales Ziel: Die Schüler erweitern ihre kommunikative Kompetenz, indem sie Fragen formulieren und diese in einem Interview stellen und beantworten.

Feinziele: Die SuS…
… wenden einfache Satzstrukturen für das Formulieren von Interviewfragen an (1).
… stellen in einem Interview vorbereitete einfache Fragen, um für sie relevante Informationen zu erhalten (2).
… geben über sich Auskunft, indem sie in der Rolle eines Sportlers Fragen beantworten (3).
… erfassen das Wesentliche von kurzen und einfachen Aussagen ihres Interviewpartners und notieren diese (4).

Thema der Unterrichtsreihe: Unit 4: Sport is good for you
Thema der Unterrichtsstunde: Fragen stellen und beantworten – An interview
Kompetenzzuwachs: kommunikative Kompetenz – Fragen stellen und beantworten

Fachlehrerln:
Material: Folie mit Fragetypen, character cards, AB questions card, AB interview, Hilfskarten zur Differenzierung

Phase	Inhaltliche Aspekte und geplante Lehreraktivitäten	Schüleraktivität Die Schüler …	Sozial-form	Me-dien/Material	Lernziele
1 Begrüßung und Einstieg 9.45-9.50	L. begrüßt Schüler. L. startet eine Fragekette mit verschiedenen Fragetypen. L.: *Have you got a brother?*	…stellen einem Mitschüler eine Frage. …beantworten eine Frage eines Mitschülers. …aktivieren ihr Wissen über die Verwendung der verschiedenen Fragetypen und deren korrekte Beantwortung. …bringen eigene Interessen in den Unterricht ein.	UG	OHP	
Gelenkstelle	L.: *Today we will learn how to interview a famous athlete. First you will find possible questions for an interview and then you will do interviews with your partner.*	…hören der Lehrperson zu. …erfahren, wie die Unterrichtsstunde aufgebaut ist.	LV		
2 Erarbeitung 9.50-10.00	L. verteilt das 'question card' AB und initiiert gemeinsames Lesen der Aufgabenstellung, gibt Raum für Rückfragen. L. legt blanco 'character card' auf OHP. L. gibt Zeitvorgabe (8 Min). L. beobachtet Arbeitsverhalten der Schüler und steht für Nachfragen zu Verfügung.	…erfassen die Kategorien auf der blanco 'character card'. …formulieren anhand der 'character card' Interviewfragen und schreiben diese auf. …nutzen ggf. die Hilfskarten mit vorformulierten Frageanfängen, um eigene Fragen zu formulieren. …vergleichen ihre Interviewfragen mit ihrem Sitznachbarn und ergänzen ggf..	EA PA	blanco 'character card' (OHP) AB question cards	1
3 Sicherung 10.00-10.10	L. legt 'character card' von Cristiano Ronaldo auf. L.: *Let's collect your questions on the board now. Please check your questions, correct them and add new questions to your list. Let's interview Cristiano Ronaldo. What can be the first question?* L. bittet einzelne SuS, ihre Fragen vorzulesen und an die Tafel zu schreiben; fragt nach alternativen Formulierungen. L. bittet weiteren SoS, die Frage aus Ronaldos Perspektive zu beantworten.	…schreiben mögliche Interviewfragen an die Tafel. …vergleichen, korrigieren und ergänzen ihre Fragen auf der 'question card'. …beantworten die aufgeschriebenen Fragen mit Hilfe der Informationen über Cristiano Ronaldo.	UG	'character card' Cristiano Ronaldo (OHP) AB question cards Tafel	
4 Anwendung 10.10-10.25	L. lässt 'character cards' und interview AB austeilen. *Don't start working yet.* L.: *Now we want to use those questions in an interview. You have to work with your neighbor. Who can read the task on the work sheet?* L.: *One of you is the athlete. The other one is a reporter and asks questions. Then you change roles. You have got 4 minutes for each interview.* L. bittet SuS, sich so hinzusetzen, dass sie sich wie in einem Interview anschauen können.	…schlüpfen in die Rolle eines Sportlers/eines Reporters und führen in Partnerarbeit ein Interview. …wenden die erarbeiteten Fragen in der Rolle des Reporters an, um relevante Informationen zu erhalten. …notieren in der Rolle des Reporters die Antworten des Athleten in der auf dem AB vorgegebenen Tabelle. …formulieren in der Rolle des Athleten kurze Antwortsätze mit Hilfe ihrer 'character card'.	PA	'character cards' AB questions cards AB interview Zusatzkarten	2, 3, 4

	L. beobachtet Arbeitsverhalten der Schüler und steht für Nachfragen und Hilfe zur Verfügung. L. weist schnelle Paare darauf hin, dass sie an einer Stelle im Klassenraum weitere Informationen zu ihrem Sportler finden, die sie erfragen sollen. L. weist auf Überprüfung durch Partner hin.			
Reserve	L. bittet ein Schülerpaar, ihr Interview vor der Klasse vorzuführen.	...präsentieren ihr Interview vor der Klasse. ...beobachten das Interview eines anderen Paares und können es mit ihrem Interview vergleichen.	SV	‚character cards' AB questions cards AB interview
Hausaufgabe 10.25-10.30	L. weist auf die Hausaufgabe auf der Rückseite des AB hin, erklärt diese und gibt Raum für Rückfragen.			

Question card

Questions for an interview with an athlete

1. Have a look at the character card of Mr. X.
2. Think of questions you can ask an athlete in an interview.

    Write them down with a **pencil**.

    (You can use the help cards on the teacher's desk)
3. Compare your questions with your partner.

1._____

2._____

3._____

4._____

5._____

6._____

7._____

Help card

Help

You can ask the athlete …
- … for his/her name.
- … for his/her age.
- … where he/she is from?
- … about things he likes.
- … about things he doesn't like.

Ideas for questions:
- Can you please tell me about …?
- What do you like about …?
- Describe what you … .

Mr. X

My goals:
-
-
-

I like:
-
-
-

I don't like:
-
-
-

sport:

country:

age:

Cristiano Ronaldo

sport: football
country: Portugal
age: 32

I was World Player of the Year in 2008 and 2016!

My goals:
- to play football for some more years
- to win the Champions League in 2018
- to stay fit until the end of the season

I like:
- to celebrate my goals
- listening to Hiphop before a game
- to shoot the most important goal of the game
-

I don't like:
- my own singing voice
- losing against German football teams
- people who say mean things about me

Character card

TIGER WOODS

sport: golf
country: United States of America
age: 41

I am the most successful golfer worldwide!

My goals:
- to win 4 more big golf championships
- to be fit for the next season
- to teach golf to my two children

I like:
- to hit the ball far away
- good weather on championship days
- going to the weight room to stay fit

I don't like:
- unfriendly reporters
- getting up early for training
- wet grass on the golf course

Usain Bolt

sport: track & field
country: Jamaica
age: 30

I won 8 Olympic gold medals!

My goals:
- to be famous as the fastest man of the world
- to run races until I am 50 years old
- to train Jamaican children in running

I like:
- to celebrate my victories with my best friend
- going for long runs in the morning
- reading a good book in my free time

I don't like:
- training on hot summer days
- to eat only healthy food before a race
- to talk about my family

Character card

Angelique Kerber

My goals:
- to win in Wimbledon this year
- to become number one on the world list
- to spend more time with my family

I like:
- to surprise other players with fast balls
- visiting my grandmother in Poland
- to go running with my best friend to stay fit

I don't like:
- to be far away from my family
- discussions with my coach
- being sick on a match day

sport: tennis
country: Germany
age: 29

I won the US Open and the Australian Open in 2016!

Simone Biles

My goals:
- to make gymnastics more famous
- to be as good as last year
- to become the best gymnast of all times

I like:
- to take selfies with my friends
- to relax in my own room after contests
- practicing to loud music

I don't like:
- making mistakes during contests
- to go to the weight room to stay strong
- to miss my favorite show on TV

sport: gymnastics
country: United States of America
age: 20

I won four gold medals at the Olympics in 2016!

An interview with an athlete

You are a reporter now.

You have an interview with a famous athlete.

1. Ask him/her questions from your *question card*. Write down everything you can find out about the athlete:

name:	
age:	
sport:	
country:	
his/her goals:	
What he/she likes:	
What he/she doesn't like:	

Are you finished?

Give your notes to your partner. He compares them with the character card.

AB – An interview with an athlete

Homework

Write down your interview. Use your notes in the chart (on this worksheet). Start like this:

    Reporter: What is your name?

    Athlete: My name is ... .

    Reporter: ...?

_____

_____

_____

_____

_____

_____

_____

_____

_____

_____

Zusatzkarten (Differenzierung)

TIGER WOODS

- has got two brothers and one sister
- has got a ten year-old daughter and an eight year-old son
- lives in California

USAIN BOLT

- is single
- has got no children
- is very religious

Zusatzkarten (Differenzierung)

ANGELIQUE KERBER

- started to play tennis when she was three years old

- lives in Poland

- plays tennis with her left hand

SIMONE BILES

- has got one sister and two brothers
- started to practice gymnastics when she was six years old
- lived with her grandparents when she was a child

Antizipiertes Tafelbild

An Interview with a famous athlete	Questions for an interview with an athlete	Vocabulary
1. Questions for an interview → 2. Interview	1. What is your name? 2. What is your sport? 3. Where are you from? 4. How old are you? 5. What are your goals? 6. What do you like? 7. What don't you like?	

BEI GRIN MACHT SICH IHR WISSEN BEZAHLT

- Wir veröffentlichen Ihre Hausarbeit, Bachelor- und Masterarbeit

- Ihr eigenes eBook und Buch - weltweit in allen wichtigen Shops

- Verdienen Sie an jedem Verkauf

Jetzt bei www.GRIN.com hochladen und kostenlos publizieren